This book is dedicated to my grandsons, Ben and Travis.

One morning, Ranger Ted was reading the newspaper in the zoo office. The phone rang. "The oldest capybara in the zoo is missing from its cage!" exclaimed one of the staff members.

Ranger Ted immediately alerted the entire staff and ran down to the capybara's cage.

All Ranger Ted could see were ten star-like footprints outside the cage. All of the other capybaras were still inside.

Ranger Ted quickly telephoned the director of the zoo. "A capybara is missing. No one knows where he went!"

The director was not happy. He rang the police and the press. "We will find our capybara," said the director. "Please be patient with us. If you see an animal that looks like a large guinea pig, please report it to the zoo immediately."

The whole city became concerned with the capybara escape. The mayor put up a large billboard in the middle of the city with a picture of the capybara. It read, "Have you seen this large guinea pig near your house? If so, call us at the zoo."

Newspaper headlines read, "Missing Capybara Roaming the City" and "Large Guinea Pig Goes Missing!"

The mayor made a big speech to the city council. They decided to help. "We will put posters all over the city," said the mayor.

"We will give a reward of five thousand dollars to the person who finds the missing capybara," said the city council.

Several days passed. Everyone in the city was looking for the missing rodent. Garbagemen checked alleyways and city bins. City workers looked in old buildings and ravines.

An old lady called Ranger Ted. "I saw a large capybara in my yard. It was eating my flowers and chasing my cat."

"That does not sound like our capybara," said Ranger Ted. "It usually does not eat flowers, but it likes grasses and water plants. I will come over right away to check."

A young boy called. "We saw a capybara in a tree at our school. It looked like a rooster!"

"That is not our capybara," said Ranger Ted. "It does not look like a rooster. It looks like a large guinea pig."

A crossing guard called. "I saw a capybara with pink fur crossing the street near the library."

"That is not our capybara. It does not have pink fur," said Ranger Ted. "It has brown fur."

"I saw a large guinea pig sitting on the zoo train while I was walking through the park," said a young mother.

"I will check with the train conductor," said Ranger Ted, "but it usually likes to be close to water."

"I saw a large guinea pig in a cage at the pet store," said a young girl. "It looked too big for the cage!"

"I will check with the store owner," said Ranger Ted. "Capybaras can be quite large and weigh up to several pounds."

Despite the several capybara sightings, no one could find the capybara that had escaped from the zoo.

CAPYBARA

16

Finally, Ranger Ted and his staff came up with an idea.

"Let's put some of his favorite food outside the cage and see if he will come eat it."

They put a large bowl of fruit and tree bark outside the cage. They waited and waited and waited, but nothing happened.

So, they came up with another plan.

18

"Capybaras like to wallow in the mud, so let's leave a large mud bath near the cage and see if he is interested," said one of the zoo employees. They left a large mud bath near the cage. They waited and waited and waited, but nothing happened.

"I have one last idea," said Ranger Ted. "Let's call Animal Control and see if they have spotted our capybara."

They called Animal Control.

The young lady who answered the phone was relieved to hear from them. "Yes! We have a very large guinea pig here that likes to eat fruit. It seems to like our volunteers when they come in to feed it. Is that your capybara?" she asked.

"Yes, it is!" exclaimed Ranger Ted with a sigh of relief. "I will be right there."

Ted called the director of the zoo. "We have found our capybara! I am going to get him and bring him back."

The next day, the mayor, the zoo director, and Ranger Ted went down to the capybara's cage to check on him. They gave him some fruit and a mud bath. After the citywide commotion caused by the capybara escape, they wanted to make sure he was happy, content, and secure in his cage.

CPSIA information can be obtained
at www.ICGtesting.com
Printed in the USA
LVOW05s0041090916

503821LV00023B/172/P